THE
OCEAN
IN THE
NEXT
ROOM

Also by Sarah V. Schweig

Take Nothing with You

THE OCEAN IN THE NEXT ROOM

poems

SARAH V. SCHWEIG

Jake Adam York Prize | Selected by Cynthia Cruz

MILKWEED EDITIONS

Published 2025 by Milkweed Editions
Printed in Canada
Cover design by Mary Austin Speaker
Cover artwork by Michael Correy
Author photo by Roberto Palomba
25 26 27 28 29   5 4 3 2 1
First Edition

Library of Congress Cataloging-in-Publication Data

Names: Schweig, Sarah V, author.
Title: The ocean in the next room : poems / Sarah V. Schweig.
Description: First edition. | Minneapolis : Milkweed Editions, 2025. |
     Summary: "Winner of the Jake Adam York Prize, this collection of poems
     seeks answers about how to live meaningfully in a world saturated by
     white noise"-- Provided by publisher.
Identifiers: LCCN 2024017220 (print) | LCCN 2024017221 (ebook) | ISBN
     9781571315632 (trade paperback) | ISBN 9781571317841 (ebook)
Subjects: LCGFT: Poetry.
Classification: LCC PS3619.C4927 O34 2025 (print) | LCC PS3619.C4927
     (ebook) | DDC 811/.6--dc23/eng/20240423
LC record available at https://lccn.loc.gov/2024017220
LC ebook record available at https://lccn.loc.gov/2024017221

Milkweed Editions is committed to ecological stewardship. We strive to align our book
production practices with this principle, and to reduce the impact of our operations in
the environment. We are a member of the Green Press Initiative, a nonprofit coalition of
publishers, manufacturers, and authors working to protect the world's endangered forests
and conserve natural resources. *The Ocean in the Next Room* was printed on acid-free
100% postconsumer-waste paper by Friesens Corporation.

For Francesco

Contents

THE
OCEAN
IN THE
NEXT
ROOM

1.

Toward the Great Unity

And then I went to seek The Great Unity.
Goodbye, I said, *my family,* as I left them.
I worked for a company in a municipal building.
In a hole, with my belongings, I built a home.

I was young, always returning to the municipal building,
where an iron lamp hung, a flickering vestige of history.
And when I moved my belongings in with a man and out of
    their hole,
Goodbye, my family. I'll be writing you, I'd said.

In their search for meaning, they resemble me, my family.
We want to understand the meaning of experience. Back when
    poetry
poured from me, words brought up history, and seemed to
transcend. When poetry stopped, to the idea of The Great Unity
    I clung.

Each morning, I walked my body beneath the flickering lamp,
meaning nothing. Words brought up history, and I wrote it down.
It left my memory empty, and I forgot what I meant.
I'll be writing you, I wrote, but could not bear the words.

Poetry stopped in my aging body. Now it carries what remains
of my family: the memory of my young brother, in the face of a man
visiting the home I built with another. Rarely, he flickers before me,
that boy, whom I could never fully record in poetry, in history.

I thought I'd find The Great Unity. It seems there is none.
Now I kneel down before its flickering idea, and my family
kneels down inside me. All of history brought us here.
Goodbye, I said, *my history*. And then my young brother disappeared.

The Tower

There was a tower of stone in a field of stone.
And the field of stone was the city.
And the Tower was built to sway in the breeze.
And we attended vocational universities,
where we learned to put our lives in a vise
and work them. At the top of the field,
we wore gabardine. This is why we were built.
This is why the Tower was built.

We knew what was possible by what our Director
announced through the speakers. We turned
our attention up toward the little silver sprinklers.
I often wonder what counts. I had my vise
work on my wounds until the wounds ate their way
into my prayers. It wasn't a competition *per se*
but I had a kind of game going with Christina.
It was called, Whichever One of Us Loses.

She had issues with gluten, and I turned
my face up like a coin toward silver at the first
static sputter of speakers. And when Christina
labored her eyes dry like raisins away from her lit
monitor, I wondered whether she was considered
more valuable in the eyes of the company.
Shoeless, she worked slowly in her swivel,
while I paid for my pumps to shine sole to heel.

Out by the Tower of stone, on the avenue,
I sat in the throne of the shoeshine chair,
and the shoeshine man, he called me *Ma'am*,
he soothed my black patent leather.
Every morning was identical to every other
as if the first morning had gone viral forever.
The afternoons were similar. I zipped up my sheath
to cover my scabs and looked in the mirror.

The Tower was built to weather the weather.
The sun had come into its own and settled.
The sun had accepted its fixed trajectory
of motion, also known as a dead-end position.
I ran a stick of color over my cheeks whenever
the sun came up, a meme. Backward facing,
I crossed my legs and rode trains into the city,
fitted neatly into my sheath. Fall settled in fields.

But in the stone city, the elderly sat on benches
losing memories. Once stonemen, they invested
themselves in the Tower. They sat in a throne
tended by a shoeshine man and tongue in cheek
called him Jeeves. So the women of our stone city
work to replace the elderly, and our Director granted
the women of the Tower a few months of leave.
This was the advent of the ballooning women.

Our Director, heir to the field, attended an ivy.
From him we learned that to beget the industry
that creates more industries, some authority first hath
to beget the word *beget*. It is similar with the population.

Fall came and the breeze changed and the Tower
filled and emptied, swaying. My office came and went
through the tunnel, singing the mission statement
of our company. I came home to unzip my sheath.

I came home to my wounds and worked them
to heal. I unwound with a glass of wine and released
my life from the vise for the length of a sleep.
Honest, our Director thinks of the office as family.
And after the baby bumps popped out of the other side
of something like it was nothing whatsoever,
the ballooning women came back donning pictures
of the outcomes. The women, they encouraged me,

but my skin crawled on the scar of my body.
It resisted commitment *per se* to such clotting. I wore
my sheath, like a sword, and the weapon was me.
The Director mistakenly called me Christina.
(I think when he said *family* he meant nothing by it.)
Still, the shoeshine man took my sole in his hands,
on the avenue of stone, on his knees, and gently.
Then one morning came all viral and it came time

to dismantle the Tower. Through speakers
came the voice of our Director and the staff
sang and beat on monitors led by Christina.
I held my hand up to the sun and saw light work
through it, and while we dismantled our lives,
the pristine blue the Director lorded over us was just
an effect of light cast on nothingness. I think
when he said industry he meant our obedience.

After the Tower, I settled down with a meat-
and-potatoes man who invested himself in me.
I called him Strawman because of how smoothly
he assembled the bales. I called him Scarecrow
because of how the look of him scattered the crows.
And so we retired my heels, and Solid Spud (also
so-called) and I, we ate from a bowl of meat
at the table's center. He'd undress me after dinner.

Still, I failed to work my nothing wounds,
yet felt the coin of my face was worth something.
The weeks piled and piled, and my ballooning skin
gripped tighter and tighter, unleashing uncertainty.
When he revealed his meat, who was he
to pronounce me a heathen? *Hare Krishna*,
chanted Spud, as if gaining us heaven admission.
He turned his coin heavenward: *Praise God*.

I hadn't thought he was "forward-thinking."
(It wasn't working for me.) One evening,
when I asked him his dreams, and he answered
densely, I shook him open like a box of instant
and mashed him in with the meat. Fall came.
The field emptied itself and crows settled
on a pile of bones. I took care of my balloon
with a hanger. (This is why there are hangers.)

The field of leaves is the world now,
and that blankness of boulders is chief.
My soul is a tool in the shed by which the scab
of my body lives. And I put the vise in the center
like a consulate. Still, I remember the Tower
swaying in the breeze of the city. Yes, I remember
the gentle hands of the shiner, and his skin
distressed as worn leather, nearly beautiful.

I'd forgotten about beauty. In the field,
I take a scythe to the leaves like I took care
of my balloon. I nurse my daughter,
the hanger, with the blood the field leaves on my fingers.
This is how we christen citizens in the country wherein
the cup of my wound is consulate. I pick a scar
and release a murder. I take this as an order to build
a new tower. I have no other real ideas.

Poem on My Birthday

It is almost the darkest day of the year.
We light lights in the dark.
It's a human thing, my mother would say.
It's a human thing

that giving something a name
seals it up and squares it away.
Several times in my life
I've changed my name.

Today is my birthday.
For a month, so I'm told, I was
The Baby. I went by nothing,
my parents unable

to agree. Recently, I do not believe
in Freedom. I believe Nature will
demonstrate our unfreedom finally.
I am thirty-five and thinking about the idea

of having a child.
We light lights in the dark.
I lost myself, my mother says sometimes,
about many various states of affairs:

a walk with a neighbor,
her marriage to my father. I am
skeptical of there being such a thing
as a self that one can just

lose. Still, sometimes I try
to point at my life
from the outside.
My husband and I

give each other dozens
of names. Is the question
how can a sound stand for a person?
an absurd question?

Can a word stand for a concept
in the same way a name can stand
for a person? Can a concept
have a life? Can we mourn the death

of a concept? The question isn't
what exists? The question is *what doesn't
die with us?* We light lights
in the dark. It's a human thing.

Tractatus

1.

I learned to live and write in the heart

of Virginia, the only state
without a song.

My last name,
given me paternally, means SILENT

in German. Germany is a place overseas
I've never seen.

What do people do at night
sitting in their cars parked alone in dark lots

while half-extinguished
headlights shine like jaundiced

eyes? They keep their windows up,
recline their seats, close their own

tired eyes. Here, there are ghosts
everywhere, but I don't

believe. I've only ever really loved

one of my lovers.
I've only ever written one poem.

My surname means SILENT

in a language I can't
speak. My lips are sealed.

2.

Some habits can't be broken.
My mouth is parched from smoke.

This is how
I account for love:

Does all that's lost break
even with all that's gained? Looking across

some internal skyline of past lust, aftermath
of ruins that remain, a windless landscape

of dust, love

is how I account for this.
Nothing is gained, thus,

I've gained
nothingness.

WHOM is a young woman's
barren womb. Then the surface

of the moon was made of ash,
or perhaps the moon

was always ash, perhaps ash
all the way through.

One thing's for sure: everything breaks,
but not even.

3.

I lived beside a column of light.

Between itself and an open window
across the street tonight

where curtains are drawn by swift wind
into the air outside,

twisted into themselves
and out, a mind that's been bent

doesn't know the difference.

We come in from the ocean.
We turn, in the end, to sand.

When he moved, the light moved with him.
(He changed the changing light.)

4.

In Boerum Hill,
a man barks at a dog.

Wednesday.

Go find a window through which
you might watch

the rain.

5.

I never loved.
I never murdered.

Therefore,

I loved and murdered
never. I murdered never

and forever. Two EVERs

cancel
each other as two lovers

on separate shores.

Forever after,
ever after for,

the aforementioned for
composes strewn

leftovers. See?

Even this
must end

with tangled words
and, through it,

one irrefutable
FOR.

Even this must end
with some convoluted

logic
and with

a dedication.

2.

Five Skeins

1.

Now I am making an infinity scarf
in my crumbling country. An infinity scarf is a scarf with edges
but no end. I have five skeins, spun from a herd of animals
I have never seen. Soon, they will be one united

thing. In my crumbling country every day,
people spend their lives standing in lines
to buy designer sneakers. Every day, I walk by these lines
in regular sneakers. I write this on my device on my way

to work. I work all day so my king can hunt lions.
On my device, I keep contact information
for people I love, as well as video I shot
across borders. My crumbling country still loves

borders. Because I am making an infinity scarf
in this moment, I am a Maker of Infinity Scarves.
My country loves this way of speaking. It is
a way of moving through the world without need

of thinking. I am making an infinity scarf in my crumbling
country, trying to bring these nothing-theses together.
All true words mean approximation. I am trying to make
one united thing. I have now finished the first skein.

2.

The greatest poet on Earth lives on an island.
My friend knows him. He writes poems for food.
Writes poems in his head. Writes poems on the sand
at low tide, so the sea can erase them.

The greatest poet refuses to publish
anything. On the island he lives happily.
I'm not sure if I believe my friend.
I would like to believe him

the way my crumbling country would like
to believe in borders. When I was becoming a writer
(always still becoming) I thought it enough
to cross the border of myself, to reach out and touch

another person. I was in love with someone
whose borders were always shifting. I spent my life
pursuing a treaty. Now, years later, it seems
I wasted years of my young life. It seems

the kind of thing the greatest poet on Earth would have
never done. Because he lives in absolute freedom,
begging only for food. Because he has no concerns
for borders. He is the second skein.

3.

The fall of a city is a thing I watch
thanks to advances in technology. The city is being
blown to pieces, buried in history.
Sometimes I stay up late sheerly to see

my husband sleeping, ensconced in vulnerability,
to try to imagine us living in the falling city.
This city was caught in a war because of
the usual disputes about power and borders.

I carry this city in my pocket because
that's where I carry my work. You must love
your work lest you have no life left
to love. I carry this city in my pocket because

that's where I carry my friends.
I don't know who is real and who isn't,
but entities in the device want to connect.
They send and send requests.

In my crumbling country, we listen
to the old stories we've been telling ourselves
about ourselves forever. So this
is despair. The third, terrible skein.

4.

When my friend died, I was in another country.
I took the train from one ancient city to another,
trying to read a newspaper in a language I didn't know,
an article about black holes.

The reason for the article, presumably some discovery,
was unintelligible to me. Out the window,
a volcano took almost a full hour to go by.
I would like to recede in the same way, sometimes.

Now I am making an infinity scarf
in my crumbling country. An infinity scarf is a scarf with edges
but no end. I have five skeins, spun from a herd of animals
I will never see. Soon, they will be one united

thing. I carry these words in my pocket because
that's where I carry daylight and moonlight:
Fold the fabric in half the long way,
pretty sides facing together inward.

My husband and I stood in the ruins of Rome
like everyone else. With devices, we filmed birds
flying above the ruined forum at night, the floodlights lit up
their feathered undersides. I will never be able to understand

5.

that moment. I have been working
on the infinity scarf, losing heart.
The world splays itself out before me
and I spend my life scattering myself

across its coordinates, stretching
into a constellation so complex
it loses all shape, becomes merely discrete
points of faint light, forever separate.

Pin the edges together.
I have been making an infinity scarf,
as if weaving a shroud to contain my country.
I carry these scraps in my pocket

because that's where I carry my country.
The greatest poet on Earth will never publish.
I submit this to you for publication
while my vulnerable husband

is sleeping. The greatest poet is sleeping.
My dead friend is sleeping. My king
rides his horse into the sunset
and it is perfect. *Pin the edges.*

Meanwhile in Our City of Abandon

Mango pyramids rot in Violet Market down by the ferry,
ferrying visitors back across the bay on this, the last day, shore

to shore; this, the Day of Vacation, of evacuation, the kind of day
that calls for monuments constructed of stone women and
    marble seagulls.

A last flock of starlings takes off from Dock Four, winging north,
south, northwest, their voices swallowed by distance, their wings
    becoming air.

The Grandfather Clock Tower has stopped. It will always be
mid-August, midday (12:53), and one man will always be left.

At one time, travelers arrived: tour groups formed and maps were
    dispersed.
Women held parasols and white lilies, children carried pinwheels,

and men wore fedoras above pinstripe suits. As always
in our city: perfections of landscape, sidewalk cafés, dozens

of languages spoken on streets, all understood. If beauty
is dissimilarity, as we once said, the sound of platinum bells rung

receded into each unique October evening.

Now the only citizen paces the Almond Piazza waiting
for the nonexistent waiter to bring a glass of wine, some
    conversation.

After I forged him this metropolis, skyrises fixed with silver mortar,
we relocated here where no one begs for currency, shelter, food,

or God. We took long walks down Alizarin Boulevard, we climbed
the Viridian Water Tower in the Latin Quarter, watched sunset
    with bottles of Chianti

while evening crowds below emerged into lamplit streets, discussed
the lightness of existence, expanse of history, and sometimes the
    weather,

and just above the bay I would see two moons I never
    recognized.
(They were your eyes.) If beauty is dissimilarity,

as we once said, I extract only this: his eyes as cyan, wider, less bitter.

Now the only citizen waits for night and firelight, cigarette in hand,
all trains stopped between stations, halted midtrack.

The smokestacks of the West End perfume factories
sit upon the skyline unlit.

He would speak of Derrida, I would speak of Celan
(your eyes were cyan), and we'd speak of Nietzsche's eternal return,

eternally. Once he asked me about desire (as always,
hypothetically) and the sun set before I endeavored to answer.

Meanwhile, in the Abandoned City, the water towers
have been drained. The bay has begun its slow

evaporation. The only citizen is waiting for a glass of wine.
The only citizen will await the slow fermentation, at the city's
    outskirts,

of a billion vineyard grapes.

Over us, two moons would rise and undress each other in quarters,
crescently, hip to hip. We'd lean back, light a couple of cigarettes,

echo the two plumes rising from the distant perfume factories,
    the two of us
dissimilar, if ever, as always, in the Abandoned City.

Contingencies (III)

Now, people have obtained a permit from the city
to march through the streets of the city

to protest the policies of the city.
They call it The Day of Anger.

They also call it The Day of Peace.
I sit in a seminar on Narrative & History

without speaking. Nine floors below,
people are still marching.

Sometimes, I walk the streets thinking,
Waste, Waste, Waste.

Sometimes, at the Y, I strip and enter
a room of steam. In this world,

many things reveal themselves
as incomplete. Raised train tracks look out over

concrete cubes in a work lot
stacked like toy blocks as if by God.

Now I am reading Spinoza on a white couch
bought by my husband years ago

with his ex-wife. Spinoza writes
that the mind cannot know the body

except through tenderness or pain.
I once worked at a center for Jewish history.

Genealogy institute, art gallery, archive,
reading room. The experience impressed

no lasting change or effect on my life.
Before the glass entrance I'd sit beside Gloria,

the receptionist who never looked at me.
Jenny, from the Bronx, attended coat check,

had missing teeth and a cackle laugh, and Isaiah
viewed X-rays of the contents of objects

gone through security. They were Black
and I was White, and we were careful

with each other. Now, people have stopped marching
and the usual cars traverse Sixth Avenue,

the intersection where a woman was struck
two nights ago. Sirens took her screams away.

What could we have done?
All we did was listen.

Theory of Ash

Behold the THEORY OF ASH!
shouts the woman in the public square
whose face is a carnival mask.
Some spectacle is surely about to take place.

What will you do when your mother is dead?
What will you do when your mother is dead and you come
face-to-face with the woman whose face is a carnival mask?
The Man of Good Questions asked.

What could I say to The Man of Good Questions?
I lay down with the Injured Thing in the grass.
And that's when the crowd gathered. They gathered
in refutation of all refutations. They gathered in the absence of

anything else. *What is the meaning of the THEORY OF ASH?*
The Man of Good Questions is asking now. (Ascending the stage
is the woman whose face is a carnival mask.) *I don't know,* I tell him.
I cannot even begin to describe the beauty of what is about to
    happen.

3.

Unaccompanied Human Voice

I've been walking in wider and wider circles.
So long since I've heard music, when I do I follow.

A fire escape's machine transforms a street with bubbles.
Beneath a tree a small brass band rehearses cameos.

Evenings, fireflies contend with kids' jars, breaking free
to bring darkness to the field, tiny lighthouses anchoring.

A thousand strangers ignite their phones, feeding on feeds.
If everything has meaning, nothing has meaning.

If nothing has meaning, life briefly vacates the ether,
the only music left is the sound of forks clinking.

Human equals animal. Mind equals soul. The dark heifer
again comes to me with tragic, planetary eyes in a dream.

Lamps shine in restaurants long shuttered, an image of grief.
When the dreadful stillness started, I felt a sense of relief.

When the dreadful stillness started, I felt a sense of relief.
When we heard birdsong and sirens crescendoing,

we watched trees unfolding spring leaf by leaf,
we told time by fruits in season, coming and going.

Yes, what we once called *life* was deception.
Death swept the City of Freedom like a vaccine

curing everyone of any lingering assumptions,
inverting life, moths devouring gabardine.

I dreamed of the city and woke up a wife in a city
of masks, unloading groceries with gloves.

(Without him, now where would I be?
How long have I taken for granted this love?)

Summer squash, zucchini, nectarine, avocado, leek.
The old expressions don't suffice to wear or speak.

The old expressions don't suffice to wear or speak.
In the City of Masks, we circulate, disconnected.

How strange it always was, the showing of teeth.
Now, people know me by the tilt of my head.

The dreadful stillness fully internalized,
and circles wider and wider, I walk to mark

which shops and restaurants still stand.
My soul buzzes in its body like a firefly in a jar.

Remember Berlin and Prague. Remember Naples.
Remember that one sweltering summer together

pilsner-drunk in sidewalk cafés and over canals.
All changed now. All changed to circles wider and wider.

Today's circle displayed how the weather was nice.
Half a country away, my mother circles a lake twice.

Half a country away, my mother circles a lake twice.
In a port city, my father translates ancient lines.

My mother circles, recording herons with her device.
Just now, my husband lies down to rest his eyes.

Twice daily my mother tracks various flocks.
For hours, my father troubles over translation.

My husband fears blindness, drops drops
in his eyes and lies down. What do I owe them?

For my father, it may be too late. To ask
what I owe my mother is to ask about the infinite.

To ask it of my husband is to disconnect.
He exempts me from the economy of relationships.

The fact that I belong nowhere in this world, a triviality
when he lies down and blindly reaches for me.

When he lies down and blindly reaches for me,
I think of the economy of time. It's thought

we're grateful to lease our lives away, or should be.
Into our work-issued computers, we empty out

our minds. My husband and I pour our work
into our work-issued computers, connecting

and verifying through a virtual private network
neglecting to look up and at anything for hours.

Happy to be here! Happy to help! No problemo!
Just wanted to circle back on this! Can you circle

back on this? Can you approve my PTO?
Thanks! When we emerge to walk in circles,

we bring our little devices along, just to prove
our lives have worth, our lives have use.

Our lives have worth, our lives have use.
So, come lie with me to binge-watch streams.

Stealing time is one project I won't ever refuse,
and television means more than exchanging memes.

We don't abandon algorithms till the sundown
of vagabond bands, released from notifications.

Then we lock the door behind us of the home
we did not realize we had all along been in.

This evening's circle cut through a field punctured
at its viridian center by a hard metal grate.

The sound of running water sang of infrastructure
invented so we can live with faith in the State.

We watched children practice fighting a low sun,
reminding us Nature hasn't ever once been outrun.

Reminding us Nature hasn't ever once been outrun,
the tornadoes and long thunderstorms come.

The tropical storms. Days pass before we see the sun.
I don't know if I believe anymore in freedom,

and the vagabond band is marching through,
is marching through, the vagabond band

is marching through thoughts we outgrew,
through dreadful stillness, where we now stand,

stunned. My family has long been convinced
of the truth of emotion. My family takes pride

in privileging the unproven. Unconvinced
by such feelings I walk in a circle especially wide.

The vagabond bands are marching through this poem,
seizing beauty, all too human, as if owed them.

Seizing beauty, all too human, as if owed them,
people now sit outside by the ambulance bay,

ordering scrambled eggs and, in the siren's interim,
spouting what platitudes everyone used to say.

I walk in wider and wider circles, as if I could
elude the dread I still recall and sometimes sense.

Someone's put a sign by a scrap of woods
that says GARDEN OF DELIVERANCE.

How have we so swiftly become accustomed
to the stillness we so deeply dreaded once?

What possessed someone to, those woods, rebrand?
When we *need* belief we become convinced.

Give a man a square of open air or shoddy land,
he'll put his whole mind there, beginning to end.

He'll put his whole mind there, beginning to end,
if we have a child. *Is that what you really want?*

We ask back and forth, me and my husband.
These days are mild with more movement:

a breeze comes through the open windows:
voices of neighbors, songs from tiny speakers.

Everyone carries their own music now,
as if the dreadful stillness has grown weaker.

Is that what you really want? To enter life
by creating it? To crowd thought with motion?

Having grown repute for introversion, early goodbyes,
we're like patron saints of unreturned invitations.

A song goes by this open window, up and through:
The world is gone, so I must carry you.

The world is gone, so I must carry you,
so goes the old song I used to know.

It comes to me again in dreams of caribou
who open their dark eyes in fields of snow.

Remember, years ago, we'd emerge
in the snow, when it still got cold enough.

The crunch under our boots, the surge
of drifts we'd climb, now become the stuff

of dreams, helping us grow better accustomed,
a matter of survival. Human equals animal.

I dream I'm abandoned in a hospital, holding
a newborn, masks everywhere. Mind equals soul,

as I am, constituted of fearful thinking, waking
from dreams of endless snow to endless heat, shaking.

From dreams of endless snow to endless heat, shaking,
I reach for my husband. I don't know if he's forgiven me,

but how he holds me hasn't changed since last spring.
Legally speaking, love is life and property.

Genevieve believes that in the law there's poetry.
She gave up poetry, making such belief a testament

or convenience. Each week she Zooms into therapy.
I've seen her boyfriend once and never her apartment.

From the firm, she texts me flowers and emoji heart-eyes.
I tell her I'm trying to live my contradictions,

my life a poem I keep trying to revise.
I tell her to watch *King Lear* on evil Amazon:

The weight of this sad time we must obey.
Speak what we feel, not what we ought to say.

Speak what we feel, not what we ought to say.
So long since I heard poetry that when I did,

I half remembered myself. The other day,
I was remembered of how my mother said,

in conversation, *I was remembered of*—
repeating this construction twice, over Zoom.

We were discussing *The Brothers Karamazov.*
How little I have in recent years really known

anyone. My mind rests on ancient worries as a crutch.
On a neighboring roof live two doves.

Save my gaze, their lives haven't changed so much.
A boy asks, in *The Brothers Karamazov,*

forgiveness of *birds, meadows, trees, sky,* saying,
I did not notice the beauty of it all, dying.

I did not notice the beauty. Of it all dying,
I speak too frequently. We sit outside,

drinking, watching masked strangers passing,
attempting to set worries, old and new, aside.

Tired human dramas go on, almost miraculous,
as does the tired human boredom. The sky

preps for rain, liquidates its birds like a loss
of interest. Notice the beauty. Or try.

At the neighboring table, at this sidewalk café,
a young woman discovers her boyfriend drinking

with another and confronts them, like in a play
from a bygone era, I keep thinking.

How does it fall now, the weight of conscience,
into this so-called Garden of Deliverance?

Into this so-called Garden of Deliverance,
our friends' child is born. They call her Lola June.

The photo they send reminds us of human innocence.
My iPhone tells me it's my window of ovulation.

I watch the videos my iPhone generates
of my memories: Portraits, At the Beach.

Bogotá. Naples. Berlin. Prague. Old portraits
of us in all the domed cities we now can't reach.

But was all that movement just avoidance?
Avoidance of what? What deeper truth?

I walk through the Garden of Deliverance
while our friends, packing up, fly forth

not back. My mother mails me new masks.
Are you taking a walk today? my husband asks.

Are you taking a walk today? my husband asks.
I vacuumed the floors, washed the dishes,

unpacked the groceries, the usual tasks.
I want to write a story that starts *It was*

during the dreadful stillness as if such a gesture
might suffice to put it behind us. *It was*

during the dreadful stillness when I met her,
Sam, a second time. I didn't recognize

I'd met her before until I heard her voice
from behind her mask, then saw the certain slant

of her eyes. Because of her visa, she'd had no choice
but to fly from England, stay in the apartment

of our mutual friends, and try to reenter the country.
I reached across the gate and handed her the keys.

I reached across the gate and handed her the keys,
remembering the party last fall at the apartment

of our mutual friends, when speaking was easy.
Crowded around a little table the time we spent

talking about the painting made of concrete
hanging on the wall felt somehow important.

It depicted a construction site, hollow concrete
cylinders, and I found I wasn't as hesitant

as I'd been recently to speak openly about art
and thought. I'd been unemployed, having been "let go,"

uncertain about any possible direction, apart
from art and thought. It feels a lifetime ago,

we agree. She'll help pack up our friends' belongings.
They are in Berlin, nothing keeping them from staying.

They are in Berlin, nothing keeping them from staying,
and we are in New York, uncertain what is barring us

from picking up and leaving. Some days everything
matters. Other days are other days. The luxurious

emptiness has replaced the empty luxuries.
Through open windows comes increasing chatter

indicating to me that it's time to leave.
I've been walking in circles wider and wider

and enter my dreams, where I change my shoes,
pass by a person I recognize, a tertiary character

from a show we've been streaming, whose
slow gaze meets that of the galactic heifer.

I wake to the empty chatter that's resumed.
And now, mid-August, the hibiscus has bloomed.

And now, mid-August, the hibiscus has bloomed
everywhere. *How can we re-earth ourselves?*

the acupuncture place emails. *Hands-on, operations-
oriented, long-term owner's approach to invest,*

notifies a lengthy investment prospectus.
Everywhere: language. You must try again to write

the true things: *In four months, I'll be thirty-six.*
But true things feel beyond access tonight.

*There are as many selves in one person
as places in the world.* Tonight I'm San Francisco,

burning, while someone's playing Gloria Estefan
on their fire escape in the streetlight's glow.

Quoth the Substack from the acupuncturist:
Here we are in the Golden Harvest.

Here we are in the Golden Harvest.
From fire escapes, eaves, and ledges

hang banners reminding us: *Resist.*
So long immersed in the city of empty offices

it was months before we saw an American flag
to take note of its persistent half-mast status.

Symbols may be dead in our country of branded swag,
but some still speak of Golden Harvests,

and Gardens of Deliverance. Is it enough
to remember beauty? Will it sustain us through

the bitter pain of any human endeavor and its rebuff?
By the sea, I've been remembered of my ability to

find redemption in the endless oceanscape.
(The small machine's long gone from that fire escape.)

The small machine's long gone from that fire escape,
transforming the once-empty street into a dream.

Then, an army of jet planes returns to scrape
the sky. The Garden of Deliverance turns in a storm

to a field of stumps. A single trumpeter practiced
Rhapsody in Blue out by the Deliverance

of Stumps, drowned out by drums of a passing protest,
stalked above by a chopper, news or police.

This year, I enter books like I once entered
other countries. This year, I collect friends' keys

as they leave, and return them to proprietors.
This year, I'm frequently self-deceived

in keeping this crown going, having nothing to say.
The weight of this sad time we must obey.

The weight of this sad time we must obey.
In the Deliverance of Stumps, someone

built a makeshift teepee along the pathway
from another fallen tree's splintered limbs.

Evenings: zucchini, peach, nectarine, garlic scape.
My husband cooks. We eat, watching streams.

Mornings: I escape screens on the fire escape
to see birds disperse and regroup, tree to tree.

There's a man across the yard who, each day,
opens the window to smoke, TV blaring behind.

Each morning, he puts out peanuts for blue jays
on the windowsill, arranging the shells in a careful line.

We all create little beauties as consolation for the strife,
the bitter pain of leading any human life.

The bitter pain of leading any human life
I follow, with a workout video called Batwings II,

a sequel named for what we, in our bodies, spite.
The man across the way opens the window.

The cooling sky is now scraped with flights.
The man across the way lights another cigarette.

The bitter pain of trying to escape any human life.
Today the blue jays seem to enjoy making him wait.

I can't tell if the little beauties are consolation.
I can't tell if all new art is mere amalgamation.

I know we can't ever fully fathom the pain
of being anyone else. With my two phones, in the sun,

I steal time in what was once the Garden of Deliverance.
The city's reawakening means I go chasing emptiness.

The city's reawakening means I go chasing emptiness.
I have seen this city through many different times.

It has seen me through, too, but with indifference,
and here I still am, chasing these empty rhymes.

In wider and wider circles, I've been walking
through wooden dust, over downed limbs

and skimmed lawns, and metal grates singing,
longing for renewables, through the Garden

of Deliverance, unsure who's being delivered
from what to what world and by whom.

At a hint of fall the other day, we shivered.
With my family I talked of weather over Zoom.

As the sky grows reaccustomed to flight paths,
I recount this year by its prevalence of lacks.

I recount this year by its prevalence of lacks.
I can tell this year by its absence of movement.

I can tell this year by our random acts
of laughter, in resistance to the terrific moment.

So long since I've seen my mother. So long
since I came upon a view. So long since

I heard music that when I did I followed
a succession of notes to the Garden of Deliverance.

Do what you need to do, my husband says,
to feel sane. When he speaks at the wrong time

I refuse him. I have avoided poetry for ages.
I have avoided trying to say the true things.

I wanted life to drown out the thought of art.
I'd wanted art to drown out the thought of thought.

I'd wanted art to drown out the thought of thought.
How slim a strip of forest is this Garden

of Stumps compared to the towering facades
and boulevards of the City of Freedom back when

I drank beer on rooftops and fell in love,
when I came home late on underground trains,

writing in notebooks during the transfer of
lines, the rats scurrying from sudden rain.

This isolation was a long time coming.
Already so many of my friends had left.

My mother says, over the phone, *Nothing*
for me has changed much, the warp and weft

of the depressed weaving the days seamlessly together.
It has been eight months since I've seen her.

It has been eight months since I've seen her,
my mother. It's been a whole sky emptied of flights

and filled again with scrapes since I've seen her.
Now the hibiscus has fallen, and so has the light.

When the dreadful stillness first started, I felt relief,
but each morning now I recall troubled dreams.

Someone's chasing an animal, or suddenly grief
presents itself in moth-eaten tenuous seams.

The window is open this morning and it's early.
I'm distracting myself by trying to write the true things.

A breeze comes in and lifts the red curtain, slightly
hinting at the decaying season. My husband is sleeping.

Eight months since I've seen my mother. Meanwhile,
there's a sense that missing anyone is futile.

There's a sense that missing anyone is futile
like the soundtracks of shouting fans matched

to streaming matches taking place, meanwhile,
in empty stadiums in countries we can't reach.

At first, a small makeshift team of office workers
still walked a few blocks to the subway station

then right back. We are a sort of animal clever
enough to invent games prolonging old delusions.

In the park the squirrels are burying acorns,
the nests of spring long abandoned,

and edges of trees appear singed and worn.
Our beliefs and attachments are utterly random.

A gleaming silver cup is hoisted up by the winning team.
Confetti and streamers fall in an empty stadium.

Confetti and streamers fall in an empty stadium,
an image of a human soul, if we still believe

in souls. Meantime, our lives in circadian rhythm
continue to run, bodies beneath a canopy of leaves.

Wider and wider circles now in late August,
when tired branches host the summer's last cicadas

breaking into their mechanical songs, a slow exhaust
of lifeblood, if we still believe in lifeblood.

What have we learned? That two herons nest
at the lake near where my mother lives. That we

still reach for each other when we lie down to rest.
That life is property and animals still visit us in dreams.

Leave the latent pain that's built up largely untouched.
What we take from the dreadful stillness isn't much.

What we take from the dreadful stillness isn't much
unlike what we took from the usual noise, now

bleeding back into life as if it just is life as such.
Only Nature is necessary, remember, and somehow

not even that, perhaps. We've altered everything,
even the two herons nest later in the year,

already gone are insects that resembled lightning,
and I read that sharks are coming closer to shore.

To this meaningless suffering my love and I
consider adding our genetic material.

The hormones will help, perhaps, counter my fright.
Delighted, everyone will wish us well.

We should know better, but why be any different?
We all think the way we live our lives is significant.

We all think the way we live our lives is significant.
To the Masquerade of Nothing's Changed

a bored couple invites us, bringing endless want
and sparkling wine, saying whatever they used to say,

rehearsing a laughter of unbearable lightness
as the sky turns pink over the clink

of stemmed glasses, a toast, a relentless
fest of the lost, scared, too drunk to think.

This is not the life I want now, nor was it
ever. That's one thing that hasn't changed.

Sufficiently masked, I can perform my part.
She asked how long we've been trying, if we've arranged

for every conceivable thing, calling it *magical*.
Nothing more fearful than being an animal.

Nothing more fearful than being an animal,
subjected to whims and winds of Nature.

So much data works to keep feeds forever full.
I watch videos of melting glaciers.

Again the vagabond band is marching through
the Park of Human Sounds. His head bent down

a mutt approaches, one brown eye and one blue,
his gaze seeming to recognize the humiliation

of being a living thing. An excursus a day in August,
and I don't know what it's taught or where it's taken me.

The pointless beauty of every human colossus
on my market-ready consciousness weighs heavy.

Do you know where this excursion has taken us?
I've been walking in wider and wider circles.

Waves

Here we are, in Barbados, at Waves Hotel and Spa.
We are three, now, with an infant son.
Every other guest is British, burnt pink and smoking.

The literal is all that's left.
Our son cries, and for a few long seconds
I do nothing, keep writing.

Everyone has a penchant for cruelty, given opportunity.
Between feeds, I order a "mango breeze colada."
By the highway, men selling coconuts wield machetes.

The sunset is burnt pink and smoking.
Our son needs to go down one more time before the long sleep.
He cannot speak, but screams.

My mother always says: He is taking in everything.
Implicitly: He cannot yet accuse me of wronging him.
My husband always says I always use words like *never* and *always*.

To the sound of my son clinging to waking reality
I drink in the view and a colada. Fear and worry,
fear and worry, hardening oneself to it, no escaping.

The sky is pink and smoking. The sea glints like machetes.
Another day in paradise, says the man trying to sell bracelets.
(What he must think of us!)

Maids come imperceptibly while we're at breakfast
and make our bed. Privilege is the dream of not having
to make one's bed.

The water is turquoise and azure.
The scar where our son was pulled out of me screaming
is turning a shade of burnt pink, darker and darker.

The waves at Waves are shallow but the horizon immense.
Our love for our son is immense.
Then suddenly I forget his existence.

The burning sun rises behind us and over the water sets.
The waves break and break.
In the eyes of the staff, my pale son is just another guest.

They have children of their own, somewhere else. The other side
    of the island
perhaps. Each morning at five they wake to drive here
to sweep the sand from these decks.

The literal is all that's left us, them, anyone.
It's what we've been taught, what we've been told.
The scramble of headlines is the world. We come here to forget,

throw away thoughts like the Brits the butts of cigarettes.
What will the human world look like when our son is old?
How old will he be at his death? At ours?

There is no longer any moral center. Was there ever?
Like the porous rocks that keep washing up
I want to far-fling these thoughts.

Welcome to Waves, where waves break and break
and remind us of the sleep machine we brought
to soothe our infant son. We are three now.

We hope waves inside the sleep machine move him
from waking to dreaming
seamlessly. The water is gold and cyan.

We are different than we were.
Is this your first time on the island? Are you a gold star member?
The questions come ceaselessly and we force the gracious smiles.

Is this your first time by this turquoise water?
We break like waves into laughter. Yes, this is our first child
(likely last). This time by the turquoise water will be a time to
    remember!

We hope it won't be our last! We've learned
to nod to one another rather than smile behind our masks.
How nice, everyone exclaims, that things return to normal!

Our son is referent-less and full of reverence.
Before he was born, I called him Dancing Star.
Now he smiles as if in answer.

Our room is oceanfront. We shut the doors, and set the sleep
    machine
to waves. For our son, reference preceded referent.
It's knowing the world, perhaps, that ruins us.

Our son, full of reverence, takes in everything
and weeps. It will be months before he speaks
but he makes sounds in sequence.

When he's awake I want him to sleep.
When he sleeps I miss him terribly.
My love for him is immense and contradictory.

The literal is all that's left. He sobs until he can barely
catch his breath, then drops into a dream,
smiling. Sleep comes for him. What could he accuse me of?

I go for a Waves signature scrub. On the questionnaire of
    afflictions at reception
I check "inability to turn off." The girl who works on me can't be
    more than eighteen.
Her father lives in New York, too, she tells me.

Now sleep is all I think of. When it will come for him, for us.
The inability to turn off means my husband and I *have words*, an
    expression
meaning we argue in whispers until our throats are hoarse.

We are fortunate and it is hard. Sleep and milk. Worry and fear.
It never ends, one of us always says.
Oh it will end, the other says, cryptically, as if fulfilling a pact.

Our son has no words yet.
On the walls of our room are pictures of the sea and portraits of
    shells.
Would I like a wellness juice? Would I like to add alcohol?

In the activity foyer, a local artist paints a portrait of a guest.
Between such commissions, he demonstrates painting
sunset after sunset.

What kind of world will his children inherit?
Will it resemble the one inherited by ours?
(Is the articulation of this question a patronizing gesture?)

I struggle to put our son down before the long sleep.
I forget his existence as I write, read.
I put my finger to my lips when my husband comes from the deck

into the room of sleep. The waves stop suddenly.
I remember the machine. I scramble to turn it on again.
We are different than we were.

Hotels no longer distribute pads of paper and pens.
No more stamps at customs. Everything wrapped in plastic wrap.
Why this impulse to poetry if I believe the literal all that's left?

Into this new contactless world my newborn son
opens his arms wide, and I pick him up, hold him close.
On the sizzling midday deck the Brits take long drags through
    their cigarettes.

Heat rises off the horizon like smoke.
They flick away the butts, artifacts of breath, symbols of death.
When cocktails come cherry-less they send them back.

The waves break and roll back.
We take turns creeping to and from the room of sleep.
We are three now.

Why this impulse?
Reality is not enough. It's as if I'm standing outside myself
watching myself play Mother, every gesture tenuous.

It never ends, one always says.
It isn't fair to quantify love, and yet
sometimes it's as if I don't have enough.

It's as if there's no such thing now as "as if,"
only the urgent and literal left, no time for hypotheses.
As I write each line I forget my sleeping son.

I am privileged to lose myself in words.
Here we are in paradise, privileged
to lose ourselves in the waves, sent back and back.

Despite the line of the imperceptibly rising horizon,
to swim we fly from sea to sea.
The sky turns violet and the sea turns violet as if in answer.

If it's knowledge of the world that defeats us
I have no answer. I have only this inexplicable impulse
to cling to poetry.

Perhaps poetry is just one way of processing data
among many. I turn away from my son to poetry.
I turn from my son to write about my son.

Those few long seconds I do nothing.
The inability to turn off. Now the fear and worry
pursue us everywhere. Now the water is turquoise and purple.

We are different than we were. Welcome to Waves.
Where we came so as not to break.
Where we have paid to have someone make our beds, straighten up,

sweep our thoughts away.
Where we snap and post photos instantly.
Where we sit thinking about how we cannot turn off and yet
    want to remember.

Where waves break and break, and I think of the sleep machine.
Where my infant son's cries rise up and finally
snap, until he drops.

I watch real waves and wait.
Waves stop suddenly,
and the sea and sky are gray on gray on gray,

like his eyes, full of cries, full of sleep.
How corrupted I am next to him
when he wakes up laughing.

The Blue House

I'm still here in the city I entered years ago.
I've been in the city all this time.
I don't look up and around much anymore.
I've been studying philosophy and having a son
and killing time. I follow my son from room
to room in our two-room rental. While he sleeps,
I kill a roach in the bathroom with a broom,
and even thoroughly crushed its legs keep
moving. I get up each morning still asleep
and keep moving. I've been in the city all this time
telling myself: *You are living your life.*
Years went by that I didn't notice the sky
until I glimpsed the sky in the stream of images
I thumb through from time to time. One time,
the algorithm fed me a blue house on a distant coast,
which I now cannot find. It had two bedrooms,
a yard, two decks, an unthinkable sunroom.
These days the sun burns itself out by late afternoon.
I follow my son, trying to deserve him.
In my dreams recently, birds land on my table
and die. In the stream of images, a man feeds
a mouse with a tiny spoon. Is the world this stream
of images or the trashed city I push my son through?
I've been in the city all this time, trying.
Philosophy has not prepared me. Philosophy asks:
How do I know if you're in pain?
These days, I look at my son and feel the terror
of love. And then I don't feel a thing.

Longest Night

The feeling is: Nothing fits together.
Recipes and war and discount pianos
scroll in the feed with my memories,
and I still think of my young life
as being lived in the city I left.
Every locus now has its pockets
of unfathomable wealth. Even here
I walk by a house being built
and each day there's a higher floor.
My child sleeps while others die.
Faced with the facts of this world,
the feeling is: *Refuse*, as verb
(rhymes with lose). My child sleeps
while others die. I cannot
reconcile. Even here traffic halts
when lights shoot up, like the sky
suddenly growing a spine, I later learn
are a billionaire's satellites
leaving Earth. I need a friend and time
alone. My son spends his life
with women I don't know. He's just
one year old. My algorithm plays
Classical Music for Winter. Even here
the Christmas cactus did not bloom.
I chat about a piano online
with a customer service representative
who asks me how I'm feeling
who I later learn is AI. Vivaldi comes
on next. (Obvious.) It is cold out,

and dark, so, so dark. An old locomotive,
whistle blowing, is decked out
for the season with twinkle lights,
hot chocolate for kids. A "first class"
ticket goes for one hundred. We are
the kind of animal that bequeaths
love and hatred. The moon rises
over the bay, and the feeling is
breath-taken-away. Have I told you
it's beautiful here? Have I told you
tents are everywhere? Even here,
there's a plan to "sweep" encampments,
another word for *out, out damned*
refuse, as noun (rhymes with loose),
while that house being built rises
higher and higher, the feeling being
can't-catch-a-breath at the thought
of the question of where people
will go or what they will do.

NOTES

"Five Skeins" was drafted in February 2017. While it has a wider possible meaning, the "fall of a city" is in reference to Aleppo, Syria. The "crumbling country" referenced is my own, the United States. The poem is in memory of my friend, AFB.

"Contingencies (III)" was drafted in 2014, after the police killing of Eric Garner.

"Unaccompanied Human Voice" was drafted in August 2020. The line "*The world is gone, so I must carry you*" is drawn from Paul Celan. The "passing protest" is in reference to the protests of the police killing of George Floyd.

"Longest Night" was drafted in December 2023. The line "My child sleeps while others die" is in reference to the children of Palestine.

ACKNOWLEDGMENTS

Thank you, Milkweed Editions, *Copper Nickel*, and Cynthia Cruz for seeing value in this work. Many thanks to editors of the *Cortland Review*, *Granta*, *HTMLGIANT*, the *Ocean State Review*, *PEN Poetry Series*, *Tin House*, *Western Humanities Review*, and the *Yale Review*, where some of these poems first appeared.

Many people have touched my life and challenged my mind during the years I was writing these poems; I am grateful to you all, but most especially to Roberto Palomba and Florencia Varela for your love and diligent wisdom, and to Francesco, my son, who taught me so much about being human even before he could speak. *The Ocean in the Next Room* is dedicated to him.

SARAH V. SCHWEIG is the author of *Take Nothing with You.* Her poetry has appeared in *Boston Review, Granta, Tin House,* and the *Yale Review,* among others, and her critical essays have appeared in *Public Seminar, Tourniquet Review,* and elsewhere. She works as an editor, studies philosophy, and lives in Maine with her husband and son.

The Jake Adam York Prize for a first or second collection of poems was established in 2016 to honor the name and legacy of Jake Adam York (1972-2012). York was the founder of *Copper Nickel*, a nationally distributed literary journal at the University of Colorado Denver. His work as a poet and scholar explored memory and social history, and particularly the Civil Rights Movement.

The judge for the 2023-2024 Jake Adam York Prize was Cynthia Cruz.

Milkweed Editions, an independent nonprofit literary publisher, gratefully acknowledges sustaining support from our board of directors, the McKnight Foundation, the National Endowment for the Arts, and many generous contributions from foundations, corporations, and thousands of individuals—our readers. This activity is made possible by the voters of Minnesota through a Minnesota State Arts Board Operating Support grant, thanks to a legislative appropriation from the Arts and Cultural Heritage Fund.

milkweed
EDITIONS

Founded as a nonprofit organization in 1980, Milkweed Editions
is an independent publisher. Our mission is to identify, nurture,
and publish transformative literature, and build an engaged
community around it.

We are based in Bdé Óta Othúŋwe (Minneapolis) in Mní
Sota Makhóčhe (Minnesota), the traditional homeland of the
Dakhóta and Anishinaabe (Ojibwe) people and current home
to many thousands of Dakhóta, Ojibwe, and other Indigenous
people, including four federally recognized Dakhóta nations and
seven federally recognized Ojibwe nations.

We believe all flourishing is mutual, and we envision a future
in which all can thrive. Realizing such a vision requires reflection
on historical legacies and engagement with current realities.
We humbly encourage readers to do the same.

milkweed.org

Interior design by Zoe Norvell
Typeset in Adobe Caslon Pro

Adobe Caslon Pro is a classic serif typeface with roots
dating back to the eighteenth century. Caslon was designed by
William Caslon in England. The digital version, Adobe Caslon
Pro, was developed by Carol Twombly in 1990, preserving the
elegant characteristics of the original while offering enhanced
legibility and versatility for modern digital applications.